D1300170

DREAMING WILD
In the Heart of the Pennypack

*To Abe
with Warm Regards
Feodor Pitcairn*

PHOTOGRAPHY BY
FEODOR PITCAIRN

Text by Mary C. & David J. Robertson

Introduction by Leslie Sauer

GIVING BIRTH TO A BOOK OF COURSE is not a solitary effort. I have special gratitude for Mary and David Robertson, whose support, writing, and organizational skills have proven essential. It has been a delight to work with them.

I am also grateful for the support of the Board of Directors of the Pennypack Trust and the many members and friends of the Pennypack who have helped this dream to come true.

Feodor Pitcairn

©MMII by Pennypack Ecological Restoration Trust

Pennypack Ecological Restoration Trust
2955 Edge Hill Road
Huntingdon Valley, PA 19006-5099
215.657.0830
pert@libertynet.org
www.libertynet.org/pert

All rights reserved, including the right to reproduce this book or parts thereof in any form, except for brief quotations in a review.

Published by the Pennypack Ecological Restoration Trust in cooperation with The Covington Group, Kansas City, MO.

Hardcover ISBN 0-9726381-0-5

Photography by Feodor Pitcairn
Text by Mary C. and David J. Robertson
Book design by John Goschke

Printed in Korea
The Covington Group
www.covingtongroup.net

INTRODUCTION

Leslie Sauer

THE PENNYPACK PRESERVE IS EMBLEMATIC OF THE JOURNEY that a landscape and a caring community can make together, beginning as a place to start an intentional community, and today, confronting the inseparability of community and place.

These urban woodlands are some of the most ravaged of landscape fragments, the first forests cleared and the longest occupied. Here we face the future, a future of our own making where the once complex forests of our almost remembered past are largely in a state of ecological collapse today.

The managers of these urban forests have led the way toward an understanding about managing the future environments of our developed landscapes. While most scientists were going ever further afield to find "pristine" landscapes to observe, a few dedicated their efforts to the most serious ecological problems we have created at home. Research conducted in the Pennypack Preserve documents both impacts as well as strategies for restoration, including soil amendments to mitigate soil eutrophication and enhance regeneration of native species, deer monitoring and management programs, invasives control and reforestation techniques.

In fact, the Pennypack demonstrates a new approach to preserved land, where the steward actively intervenes to sustain the values inherent in the landscape rather than merely corralling them in a fenced off area. Protection from development has not been enough to conserve biodiversity in our scattered preserves.

There can be few efforts more difficult than seeking cultural change. The Pitcairn family has supported a remarkable effort by the people of this community to shift the path that we are taking, away from an increasingly impoverished environment towards a sustainable future and a legacy of richness to pass on to our children. As has been noted before, and by others, environmentalists make good ancestors.

This effort, begun by the Pitcairns and continued by the Pennypack, was ahead of its time when the organization was a watershed association and it is still ahead of its time as the organization takes on the mantle of a land trust dedicated to stewardship. I am quite confident that sometime in the future people will look back and recognize the Pennypack Preserve as one of the pioneer projects in forest restoration, along with Wissahickon Park in Philadelphia, and Central Park and Prospect Park in New York City.

These photographs represent the best this forest has to offer at this moment in time. They are a record of a gift to us that only the future will tell if we pass along to our grandchildren. **P**

DREAMING WILD
In the Heart of the Pennypack

Mary C. & David J. Robertson

O**N THE 22ND OF JUNE 1969,** on the fringe of downtown Cleveland, Ohio, in the area known as The Flats, an oil slick on the Cuyahoga River caught fire and damaged two railroad trestles.[1] The event did not generate much immediate attention, but by August when *Time* magazine featured the story, the oxymoronic image of water burning drew far greater notice. The attention at this point was a bit unusual, however. After all, the river had burned before in 1952 and that fire had caused 30 times the damage of the 1969 episode. In addition, the event took place in a heavily industrialized section of the river where river traffic with its attendant petroleum pollutants helped keep the heartbeat of Cleveland industry going. Still, the idea of water so fouled that it could burn, blackened the city's image and prompted city officials to focus more intently on pollution issues.

Meanwhile, a state away in southeastern Pennsylvania, the Pennsylvania Fish and Boat Commission in 1969 refused to stock trout in the Pennypack Creek for a second year in a row. Although the creek is a Delaware River tributary, its size didn't allow for commercial traffic and much of its upper reaches remained nestled in bucolic countryside. In fact, according to a February 14, 1971, *Philadelphia Inquirer* article, at one time the creek was clean enough to sport eight fishing holes in Philadelphia. So, if Pennypack Creek wasn't an industrial workhorse in 1969 like the Cuyahoga River, what had happened to bring the creek to such a state?

Birth of a Creek

The roots of Pennypack Creek's predicament actually stretch unimaginably far back in time—a third of a billion years.[2] At that time, Africa was roughly sutured to eastern Pennsylvania along a scar of mountains towering as high as the modern Rockies—the ancient Appalachians. The familiar terrain of today's Pennypack valley lay buried beneath many thousands of feet of tortured rock that had been crumpled and bulldozed onto the edge of the continent as Africa collided with North America in slow motion.

---

1 Case Western Reserve University's website, "The Cuyahoga River Fire: June 22, 1969," on which this information is based, features a retrospective of the fire and links to contemporary *Plain Dealer* and *Cleveland Press* newspaper articles.

2 Two chapters in *The Geology of Pennsylvania* chronicle the geologic history of the Appalachian Piedmont.

The continental merger lasted 40 million years until it was sundered by magma welling up from deep inside the earth. The column of hot, fluid rock rose directly beneath the mountains and spread out laterally under each continent, gradually floating and tugging Africa and North America apart. The process of splitting the continents stretched the earth's crust until, unable to stretch any further, the crust cracked into gigantic blocks. The blocks subsequently sank thousands of feet. On the surface, this cracking and subsidence produced a long, deep basin. Rivers pouring from the Appalachian heights southeast of the basin carried the sediments northwestward into the valley where they accumulated in thick layers. Over time, the rivers filled the basin with sand and mud and the growing weight of the sediments compressed the lower layers into stone. Once filled, the basin resembled a long, narrow trough made out of very hard and ancient rock filled to the brim with softer and much newer rock.

As erosion continued to reduce the height of the mountain highlands, the Atlantic Ocean was spreading open between Africa and North America. These two forces acting in concert eventually caused the flow of the rivers and streams to reverse so that, instead of flowing northwestward toward the now-filled basin, the rivers began to flow to the southeast toward the ever widening Atlantic Ocean. Because most of the material that had eroded off of the mountains and accumulated in the basin was never buried deeply enough to be compressed into really hard rock, the rivers now flowing toward the Atlantic Ocean washed sediments off the land and into the ocean very quickly. In southeastern Pennsylvania, this erosion continued until the vast majority of the debris from the ancestral Appalachians had washed away into the Atlantic and the basin sediments were worn

flush with the top of the basin wall. It was at this point, about 140 million years ago while dinosaurs roamed the earth, that the Pennypack was born.

The ancestral Pennypack and its sibling Delaware River tributaries all developed on the very hard gneissic rock making up the confining walls of the basin. This rock is among the most ancient on earth—over a billion years old—and repeated episodes of heating and compression associated with mountain building made it dense, durable, and resistant to erosion.

Because this rock is so hard, the ancestral Pennypack cut its valley very slowly. The creek likely would have been much like a mountain stream—fast, rocky, clear and cool. Once a distinct channel developed in the hard rock, though, precipitation that fell on the sediment-filled basin to the north also began to drain into the nascent creek. When the terrain from the basin finally was incorporated into the creek's watershed, the modern drainage was set. Over the millennia, the Pennypack gradually eroded more and more deeply, but the essential pattern that the region and its people have come to recognize as the Pennypack watershed was now imprinted on the land.

Because the Pennypack drains both the sedimentary basin and the hard rock of the basin walls, it assumes two distinct personalities. Through the upper reaches of the watershed, the stream courses gently over easily eroded sandstone and shale bedrock of the basin, creating shallow valleys and low, rolling hills that are characteristic of the communities of Horsham, Hatboro, and Warminster. As John McNeil points out in *Ramblings along the Pennypack*, the Native American

Lenni-Lenape who inhabited the area may have had the upper Pennypack in mind when they called the stream Peme-peck, "bear fat creek" or "water without much current"—a good name for this stretch of the creek.

Downstream, though, in the Morelands and Bryn Athyn, the stream crosses over onto the hard basin walls and its other personality asserts itself. The valley walls close in, confining the creek to a narrow, wild channel clogged with blocks and boulders. Rocks and falls alternate with deep, shadowy pools. When the creek finally emerges from its rocky ravine and spills out onto the coastal plain for the last two miles before joining the Delaware River, it resumes its languid identity akin to that in the upper watershed.

Early Land Use

Pennypack Creek's erosion through the ancient roots of the Appalachian Piedmont shaped more than the regional landscape. Not only did the stream pierce through the hard, rocky barrier separating the flat and accessible coastal plain to the south from the similarly flat and arable land of the basin ten miles inland, but it did so in a way that invited people to exploit the natural resources in the watershed.

Both Native Americans and European settlers found that the creek and its valley suited their needs well. The Lenni Lenape, the Middle Atlantic representatives of the Delaware Indian confederation, took advantage of the fish in the stream and the game in the surrounding forests. The European settlers utilized the flowing water for power, the land for farming, the forests for lumber, the bedrock for building stone, and the valley bottoms for convenient transportation.

During the heyday of water-powered milling in the first half of the 19th century, thirty mills were situated along the length of the creek and its tributaries, with seventeen of them located in Moreland Township—the modern communities of Upper and Lower Moreland Townships and the Boroughs of Hatboro and Bryn Athyn.[3] Within the boundaries of the Pennypack Preserve—the natural area owned by the Pennypack Ecological Restoration Trust (the Pennypack Trust) in the central part, or heart, of the watershed—six mills drew power from the creek between 1760 and 1885 on sites within two miles of one another. Here, gristmills, a plaster mill, a paper mill and a distillery operated. The mills fostered the construction of ancillary buildings such as owners' and workers' homes and other appurtenant structures. In fact, enough inhabitants clustered around the mills owned by George Shelmire and his family at the intersection of what are now Huntingdon and Creek Roads that the community was called Shelmire Mills.

The large number of gristmills, in particular, attests to the agricultural modifications the settlers were making to the land. Not surprisingly, agriculture was an important part of early settlements and wheat was a favored crop. The gristmills ground the wheat into flour and were especially convenient for those farmers living in the watershed who transported the grain in animal-drawn carts using roads that descended steeply into the valley and ran alongside the creek to connect the mill communities. The plaster mill probably also milled bones but both served as fertilizer, indicating the extent to which the land had already been extensively cultivated by the mid-1800s. In addition, most grist mills had saw mills attached and these transformed the forests into lumber,

---

[3] The history of water-powered milling along the upper Pennypack can be found in articles by Robert J. Walter and by Mildred Wintz and her colleagues.

both for local use and export, and firewood. The formerly wooded valley opened up more and more, encouraging the further expansion of farming.

Photograph courtesy of Steven Silverman

Fetter's Mill, typical of the series of water-powered mills located along the valley bottom, served the growing agricultural interests within the watershed and beyond.

Even the rock responsible for creating the rapids and falls that made milling possible and profitable in the valley—the ancient wall of the basin—was not immune to exploitation. Five hard rock quarries operated along the creek's banks in the central watershed where the stream's erosion had

exposed the underlying bedrock. Some of the quarried stone found its way into local structures like the cathedral in Bryn Athyn, but much of the stone was carried away from the valley on flatcars traveling on a rail bed built paralleling the creek.

The Railroads' Impact

During the era of rapid railroad expansion following the Civil War, two companies competing for the New York-Philadelphia rail traffic built perpendicular rail lines in the Pennypack valley, one heading northward and the other eastward from Philadelphia. The company building the northern line found, though, that the hard rock of the area and the hilly topography north of the city stymied construction. Engineers sought routes that offered gradual inclines and minimized construction costs, but were faced with steep hills that could only be excavated by blasting into the resistant rock. So, instead, they chose to route the railroad through natural excavations that had been ages in the making— stream valleys like the Pennypack.

The Philadelphia, Newtown and New York Railroad Company (later acquired by the Reading Railroad) built its line to link Philadelphia with New York City through Newtown, which was then the county seat of Bucks County. This line paralleled Pennypack Creek through the deepest and most tortuous portions of the creek's ravine. Even though the engineers chose the easiest route, construction still required the company to fill in the lower ends of many small tributary valleys, span the creek with four bridges, and blast several deep rock cuts to accommodate the tracks before the line emerged onto the gentler landscape of the sedimentary basin to the north.

To minimize costs, the rock cuts were no more than narrow chutes just wide enough to accommodate the rail cars, a configuration that had unforeseen and tragic consequences.[4] One of the cuts was built on a curve, with the result that locomotive engineers could not see far ahead along the track. In December 1921, two trains collided head-on inside this cut, killing 27 passengers and crewmembers and injuring 70 others. Most victims died in a conflagration ignited by the gas lighting system then in use in the wooden rail cars that piled up inside the cut. The inferno ensured that the cut would henceforth be known as "Death Gulch." Newspapers from Pennsylvania to California carried the story, including the comment that "there could be no worse spot in the United States for two trains to meet head-on." In the aftermath of the catastrophe, the Interstate Commerce Commission recommended major changes in passenger railcar construction that, fortunately, were adopted before 1964 when the cut was the scene of a second accident—a derailment that left five injured, but none seriously.

The arrival of the railroad hastened the demise of the few mills that remained in the valley. In fact, a portion of the Newtown line was built on fill that buried one of the mill sites, by then just an abandoned ruin. By the Civil War, most of the mills were no longer profitable. Deforestation of the watershed had made water supplies in the creek unpredictable, with muddy torrents in the wake of each rainstorm and long periods of low flow because of declining groundwater levels. In addition, the advent of the steam engine meant that power was portable and no longer confined to temperamental, flood-prone bottomlands.

Photograph courtesy of Steven Silverman

By the time the cornerstone for the Bryn Athyn Cathedral was laid in 1914, large construction timbers needed to be brought to the site by rail rather than logged locally. This photograph depicts horse drawn carts hauling the timber to the site as well as the remnant stands of forest in the creek floodplain and rocky slopes that were probably unsuitable for agriculture.

Photograph courtesy of Steven Silverman

Over eons, stream erosion had exposed the hard, gneissic bedrock prized for building stone. At times, five quarries operated in the heart of the Pennypack north of Welsh Road.

---

4 Details on the accidents along this section of rail were recounted in articles by J. Adi-Kent in *The Sunday Philadelphia Bulletin Magazine* and by J.J. McMahon in *The Philadelphia Bulletin.*

The railroads were built to capitalize on the growing and lucrative passenger and freight market between Philadelphia and New York City, but the trains also stopped at smaller communities along the route, fostering growth in those towns. In addition, the railroads subsidized the development of parks along the routes, which allowed city-bound residents

UPPER This train crash occurred on December 5, 1921, when an inbound train to Philadelphia collided with an outbound train. The accident happened because the outbound train was supposed to wait on a siding for two early morning inbound trains to pass; however, due to communication problems, the outbound train left the siding before the second inbound train had passed through. Unfortunately, engineers driving the opposing trains along this section of the Philadelphia-Newtown Line had limited sight distance as they entered the curve in a deep rock cut, making the accident almost unavoidable.

LOWER The relative isolation of the area, the rugged terrain and narrowness of the rock cut limited rescuers' ability to help survivors of the wreck.

to enjoy a day or weekend in the country. Alnwick Grove along the Pennypack was just such a park, boasting picnic pavilions, a bandstand, canoe rentals, and a swimming beach in summer and ice-skating in winter. Visitors liked what they saw, and the railroads provided the opportunity for people not only to relax in the country but also to move into the suburbs and to commute to the city to work. At first, the exodus was slow and growth was centered on established communities like Willow Grove and Hatboro where commuters could walk to the railroad station. As a result, most of the valley retained its bucolic character.

Photograph courtesy of Steven Silverman

Photograph courtesy of Steven Silverman

Photograph courtesy of the Academy of the New Church Swedenborg Archives

Physically devastated by increasingly frequent flooding and financially undercut by steam power, the valley's water-powered mills were nearly all abandoned and falling into ruin by the time of the Civil War. Some mills, like Fetter's Mill, have been restored but most have all but disappeared. The ruin in this photograph, for example, is no longer evident.

Pastoral by Design

Somewhat paradoxically, growth spreading outward from Philadelphia bypassed the central part of the Pennypack valley and jumped to the northern reaches of the watershed. This pattern was largely the result of the actions of Pittsburgh industrialist John Pitcairn. In the late 19th century, Pitcairn moved to Huntingdon Valley where he and fellow followers of the teachings of 18th century philosopher Emanuel Swedenborg purchased 1,216 acres in the central Pennypack Creek valley with the intention of establishing a religious community named Bryn Athyn, "the hill of cohesion."

With control over the property, the small group made far-reaching decisions governing the use of their land that included the creation of carefully planned residential and institutional zones surrounded by farms and estates. In contrast to the spreading development in the rest of the watershed, the new community was characterized by residences and institutions located near the train station, with diminishing population density throughout the rest of the village as the woods and fields regrew and numerous small farms were consolidated into larger farms. In some areas, farmhouses were demolished and their fields were allowed to revert to woodlands. In others, farming continued, but residences and other buildings were removed. In a few instances, small forested tracts and woodlots remained intact on knobs too rocky to cultivate or valleys too wet to plow. These remnant stands of old-growth forest served as nuclei and seed sources around which grew the new woodlands that began to re-carpet the valley's slopes.

As the population in parts of the Pennypack watershed grew, land development did also. Besides homes for people, other structures built to accommodate the needs of an increasing population such as schools, restaurants, gas stations, and convenience stores overran the landscape. Among the consequences of development were a lowered water table, the disappearance of small tributary streams, and increased run-off from paved surfaces. Even the infrastructural expansions designed to support a growing population could not keep pace.

Photograph courtesy of Steven Silverman

The Philadelphia-Newtown Line crossed the Pennypack on a covered wooden bridge just north of the Bryn Athyn Station and Alnwick Grove. Skaters in the winter and canoeists in the summer enjoyed the year 'round recreational opportunities the area provided.

The Creek Hits Its Nadir

Following the Second World War, with the completion of highways like the Pennsylvania Turnpike, the suburbs burgeoned and quickly engulfed the communities that had been the traditional transportation hubs. Joseph Dunphy, in a *Philadelphia Inquirer* article on January 17, 1971, reported that during the 1960s, the population more than doubled in the northeastern portion of Philadelphia drained by the Pennypack and in adjacent Bucks County, while Montgomery County reported a sizable gain of 22.5 percent during the decade.

This is why, by 1968, Pennypack Creek had come to be in its deplorable state. Poorly treated sewage discharged into the creek had so reduced the level of dissolved oxygen in the water that fish could not survive. A slight improvement recorded in 1969 was not sufficient to persuade the Fish Commission to reconsider its decision not to stock the creek. Dunphy noted that the most overburdened facility was the Upper Moreland-Hatboro Joint Sewer Authority treatment plant that had recently been expanded ten-fold to accommodate demand in the upper watershed and now discharged some 4 million gallons of wastewater into the creek each day—half its summertime flow.

Photograph courtesy of Steven Silverman

Floods grew in frequency and intensity as settlers cut the forests in the valley, but development in the upper watershed compounded the problem significantly. In 1938, floodwaters rose as high as the Fetter's Mill Bridge in Bryn Athyn.

Though the creek's woes had been recognized even before the Fish and Boat Commission's drastic action, efforts to effect significant change proved fruitless because such endeavors were largely uncoordinated. Stream cleanup campaigns and small, locally focused citizens' groups were unable to address the larger issues that threatened to overwhelm the entire watershed.

Concerted Efforts at Conservation

Of course, these issues were not unique to the Pennypack, but affected, to a greater or lesser extent, all of the tributaries of the rapidly urbanizing lower Delaware River valley. In response, the interstate Delaware River Basin Commission established a Watershed Planning Operation to foster the development of watershed planning organizations for all of the streams tributary to the Delaware River. This comprehensive, regional approach attracted the attention of John Pitcairn's grandson, Feodor Pitcairn, and several conservation-minded neighbors who saw in watershed-based planning the opportunity to produce real improvements in the valley. In November 1970, the group formally incorporated as the Pennypack Watershed Association.

The watershed association quickly developed a program with four interrelated objectives: pollution abatement, flood control, open space conservation, and increased environmental literacy. Within five years of its founding, the organization had made real and measurable progress. For example, the Association joined with the Department of Environmental Resources and the Fish and Boat Commission to press the Upper Moreland-Hatboro Joint Sewer Authority to upgrade the quality of effluent discharged from its treatment plant. Similarly, the Association collaborated with the U.S. Army Corps of Engineers to identify the most flood-prone parts of the watershed and to develop strategies to avoid increased flooding in the future. Members of the Association's professional staff reviewed development plans in each municipality in the watershed to minimize the impact of building on the environment. Perhaps most importantly, though, the Association adopted

During the long period when farms operated in the watershed, cattle and sheep raised in pastures on the slopes of the valley were free to graze the native wildflowers and shrubs in the remnant woodlands. All grazing ceased within a decade of the acquisition of the first land for the Pennypack Preserve.

watershed. As a result, the Association was able to devote more attention to open space conservation, securing 365 acres within a decade of dedicating the first parcel of land—no mean feat given the active competition from developers.

One notable event that underscored the Association's success in promoting environmental action occurred in 1983 when the three municipalities within whose boundaries the Pennypack Preserve is located all mutually agreed to abandon sections of two public roads that ran through the natural area. This decision was hard-won because the roads shortened local residents' commutes and they had reputations as secluded "lovers' lanes," making them sentimentally popular. In practical terms, abandoning the roads removed public vehicular traffic from the heart of the preserve. Limiting access also eliminated short-haul trash

a Pennypack Watershed Corridor Master Plan that, for the first time, proposed setting aside as the Pennypack Preserve the most environmentally sensitive portions of the Pennypack valley.

Vigilance, persistence, and cooperation paid off. The quality of the Pennypack Creek gradually improved and municipalities began to take their responsibilities for managing growth more seriously, especially in areas directly bordering the creek and in the floodplains. With greater public awareness came a general commitment to safeguarding the environmental quality of the

dumping, then a perennial and growing problem. In less pragmatic terms, though, the decision to abandon the roads and to allow them to become the backbone of the preserve's trail system was a tacit acknowledgement by the municipalities that "nature" had become a greater—and permanent—priority.

Despite all that the Pennypack Watershed Association had accomplished, by the end of the 1980s something still seemed to be slightly askew. In setting aside land for preservation, the Association hoped that the natural processes that allow fields to revert to forests would help the land to recover, which seemed a perfectly reasonable assumption in light of the woodlands that had already reclaimed the pastures and croplands of the 1920s. However, in assessing the land that it had preserved, the Association found the woods were just a little too green and the deer that everyone enjoyed seeing were becoming awfully common. As a result, the Association took a step back, just as it had when it first incorporated, in order to review the big picture. As it turned out, at the same time that the white ashes, tuliptrees and hickories were re-establishing themselves, other plants were also taking advantage of the opportunity to gain a foothold in the area, but these plants were not native to the meadows, marshes and forests of the region. In addition, residential development surrounding the preserve was squeezing deer into increasingly diminished habitat. The land that the Association had acquired was preserved in terms of size, but the natural features of the landscape were looking increasingly less natural.

While white-tailed deer are native to the valley, their overpopulation due to the lack of natural predators and shrinking habitat threatens forest regeneration. Here, a doe enjoys a native goldenrod.

Embracing Ecological Restoration

In response, the Association decided to revisit its goals, ultimately redefining its mission and emerging from the process as the Pennypack Ecological Restoration Trust. One significant outcome was that the organization readjusted its relationship to the land that it had acquired. When the Pennypack Watershed Association originally acquired land, it operated with the same goal as other environmental organizations and even national parks, that is, acquire natural lands to protect them from degradation and development. What slowly became clear, however, was that such acquisition attempted to fix the land in the moment—to freeze time, as it were. At Pennypack, as elsewhere, attempting to rely on the demonstrated success of forest regeneration was tempting, but ignored the fact that the preserved land was not a hermetic system and was increasingly affected by problems that had been set in motion long before conservation efforts began in earnest.

Thus, even as trees grew and matured, non-native, invasive plant species established footholds and thrived. Out of their native contexts, these species faced little competition, gained an enormous advantage over the native vegetation, and thoroughly disrupted the dynamic system of checks and balances that native species had evolved over millennia. The consequences stared back. Non-forested areas, for instance, were overwhelmed and blanketed by species like multiflora rose (*Rosa multiflora*). Originally introduced from eastern Asia to function as "natural" fencing between farm pastures and as wildlife habitat, multiflora rose so spread and invaded other areas that it led journalist George Laycock to dub it the "pasture snatcher." The sunny edges where woodlands met fields proved irresistible to the likes of porcelainberry (*Ampelopsis brevipedunculata*), an aggressive vine that uses the trees as a natural trellis to grow deadly curtains of green that block sunlight and thereby starve the host trees. Inside wooded areas, other vines like Japanese honeysuckle (*Lonicera japonica*) and Asiatic bittersweet (*Celastrus orbiculatus*) that tolerate shade, sprawled across the forest floor and scrambled up and over shrubs and trees. Even seemingly benign introductions into already tamed landscapes had impacts beyond their boundaries. Five-leafed akebia (*Akebia quinata*), a horticultural groundcover, broke out of gardens and into adjoining natural areas where it suffocated native woodland wildflowers and climbed dozens of feet into the forest canopy.

In the literal shadow of these and other problems, the Trust came to understand that acquisition would only be part of a larger enterprise of preservation, one that involved active stewardship. The Trust also recognized that it had the opportunity to be a leader in this field.

With the recognition of the essential role of stewardship in conservation came the dilemma over the goals of stewardship. To what end would the land be managed? The answer that emerged—ecological restoration—begged another question: restoration to what? The temptation is to say that the goal of restoration is to return the preserve to wilderness to the greatest extent possible. Certainly this idea is seductive. The concept of wilderness is deeply embedded in the American psyche. The idea of a frontier with wilderness goes hand in glove with Americans' definition of ourselves, our notions of ingenuity, individualism, and perseverance. However integral to our national identity that wilderness has become, the Trust realized that, in practical terms, "wildness" needed to be approached more pragmatically and less romantically.

As Henry T. Lewis observed in the book *Before the Wilderness: Environmental Management by Native Californians*, "among a number of ecologists, foresters, parks officials, and others there is the recognition that the 'wilderness' found by Europeans—what Longfellow erroneously referred to as the 'forest primeval'—was, in most parts of the continent and in varying degrees, a human artifact." He offered evidence in California that this artifact was the result of active aboriginal management, including the use of fire. Where native people settled, tree ring analysis demonstrated that fires occurred far more frequently than could be explained by lightning strikes. In particular, according to ecological anthropologist Kat Anderson, fire was used extensively to create second growth vegetation that yielded the materials needed for making the baskets essential for everyday life. Unmanaged, the vegetation produced useless growth, while areas managed with fire produced "long, straight, slender switches with no lateral branching" quite unlike the tangled and gnarled natural growth. In his *Synopsis of the History of Upper Moreland and Willow Grove,* Joe Thomas noted that there are records of Indian tribes converging on Philadelphia between 1750 and 1764 in large numbers to "camp for several weeks at a time in various parts of the Manor [of Moreland], particularly in the woods around Hatboro, spending most of their time in making and selling baskets, mats and splint brooms." Clearly, active land management by native peoples was not confined exclusively to the western part of the continent.

The reality is that we have created the wilderness we know more often than we realize. The lower Yosemite Valley is a case in point. Helen McCarthy compared photographs of the famous view into the valley from Union Point. One view, taken in 1866, shows a sparsely vegetated landscape, rocky and jagged. The other view, taken a century later in 1961, shows the same landscape with a far greater number of trees that have the effect of "softening" the look and feel of the land. The irony is that the "wilder" looking landscape of 1866 was actively managed by Native Americans and the "tamer" landscape is the result of the valley's incorporation into a national park which allowed the land to revert to forest again.

A Reconsideration of Wild

With this information in hand, it only makes sense to reconsider appropriate restoration goals. A good starting point would be to reconsider the meanings of wild. For urban and suburban natural lands, wildness can never be synonymous with wilderness because many of the keystone species—those animals and plants that truly define the character of a natural area—cannot survive permanently in small fragments of an ecosystem. For example, wolves, mountain lions, or bobcats will never inhabit the Pennypack valley as long as it is only an oasis in the midst of megalopolis, and people would never tolerate predators so close even if the habitat were suitable.

So we must moderate our expectations and grant that wildness has returned when nature's rules, not ours, are once again dominant. Human activity is not necessarily anathema; after all, if only land where people are completely excluded is considered wild, then no place on Earth now (and few places that we thought of formerly) could be called wild. But for wildness to reign, human activities must meet the test proffered by Aldo Leopold: "A thing is right when it tends to preserve the integrity, stability and beauty of the biotic community. It is wrong when it tends otherwise."

University of Minnesota ecologist David Tilman has elaborated on this concept throughout his long and distinguished career, repeatedly demonstrating that natural areas supporting a large and diverse suite of native plants and animals are far more stable than areas whose collection of species is less diversified. Tilman's long-term research on prairies in the Cedar Creek Natural History Area in Minnesota demonstrated the resiliency and stability of diverse natural prairies in the face of stresses such as drought compared to those prairies whose diversity had been experimentally reduced.

The opposite may be said of "American Gulch," a moniker bestowed by Ukrainian botanists on a ditch in a forlorn railroad-switching yard in Kyiv, Ukraine. American Gulch has the distinction of supporting a depauperate collection consisting of only six plant species, all of which are native exclusively to North America. American Gulch is illustrative because it's easy to imagine the consequences if a leaf-eating insect or a disease that is specific to one of these six plants were to make its way into Ukraine and find these plants: this community could be altered completely and very quickly.

Although American Gulch is an extreme example and one that could hardly be called wild, the overwhelmingly destabilizing effects of invasive species throughout the world have become widely recognized. While newly introduced species initially increase the diversity of the ecosystem, the more aggressive of the invaders so physically overwhelm the habitat that, in the long run,

In areas heavily colonized by invasive plants and supporting dense deer populations, forest regeneration has become almost impossible without aid. Deer browse the tender new growth of emerging trees while invasive plants crowd out new trees by blocking sunlight. The Pennypack Trust uses tree shelters to protect newly planted trees from damage by deer, and maintenance around the shelters eliminates competition from invasive plants.

the biodiversity of the system suffers. Furthermore, the native species that survive, not having evolved with the foreign invaders, may be unable to use the introduced species for food or shelter. In extreme cases, the invasive species may actually be toxic. The Pennypack Trust has dedicated itself to the stewardship of the natural lands at the heart of the Pennypack, which means restoring the ecological integrity of the natural areas and minimizing the influence of introduced species.

Clearly, what the Trust has learned has much to offer to the countless other natural area managers who are confronted with similar challenges.

A reconsideration of the nature of wild offers other advantages. One is that wild becomes accessible in a way that it has always been for some cultures. Roderick Nash in *Wilderness and the American Mind* made this point when he quoted Standing Bear of the Ogalala Sioux: "'We did not think of the great open plains, the beautiful rolling hills and the winding streams with tangled growth as 'wild.' Only to the white man was nature a 'wilderness' and…the land 'infested' with 'wild' animals and 'savage' people.'" Greater accessibility also means that seemingly overwhelming problems can be broken down into manageable parts and individually circumscribed. An overarching problem may take time to resolve, but if it has been divided into manageable units, the entire problem can eventually be tackled over time. As a result, people can see the results of their own direct actions. Too often environmental problems seem insurmountable for ordinary citizens' actions to have any meaningful effect, and even very practical efforts like recycling do not lead to obvious visible results. Investing a morning's efforts in promoting the wild, in contrast, by cutting vines from trees or planting a new woodland can be immensely satisfying precisely because the results are so tangible and the implications so readily imaginable.

A few other organizations like the Pennypack Trust are working to re-establish or restore the wild locally. The Pennypack Trust has worked with them to learn, and has also functioned in a teaching role by demonstrating how natural processes can be re-introduced and disruptive processes interrupted in relatively small areas, areas that are scaled to the human consciousness. Large-scale projects such as the restoration of the Everglades or the conservation of the South American rainforests, for example, are few and far between and are so overwhelming that roles for ordinary people are difficult to identify. Large changes, though, can happen through cumulative action on the smaller, more intimate spaces that most people encounter.

Dreaming Wild

Throughout most of human history, the banks of the Pennypack were so sparsely settled that people noticed the wild in the area's natural features. Even as farms and man-made structures increasingly domesticated the landscape, the wild still persisted. Where these wild elements occur, that is, where natural processes act on native species, the landscape holds sway over us. Especially where such wild lands are rare and precious, they evoke a kind of reverie, a dreaming wild. At Pennypack, these dreams take on a concrete substance.

The images in this book represent at once the very physical quality of the landscape and simultaneously so much more. Many offer the wild dream as well. In capturing the physical nature of the area, the images capture a moment in time, the landscape in transition from its domesticated recent past to a wilder future, the warts as well as the partly realized promise. However, because any photograph is the result of some decision, the images offer more than just reality. The angle, the lighting, the frame, even the choice of subject reveal to some extent the photographer but also some quintessential quality of the subject. In these images one can see some of the problems, but also appreciate the reverie at the heart of the Pennypack, the dreaming wild, that the area evokes.

Literature Cited

Adi-Kent, J. "The Wreck That Named 'Death Gulch.'" *The Sunday Philadelphia Bulletin Magazine*. 9 June 1968.

Anderson, Kat. "Native Californians as Ancient and Contemporary Cultivators." *Before the Wilderness: Environmental Management by Native Californians*. Ed. Thomas C. Blackburn and Kat Anderson. Menlo Park, California: Ballena Press, 1993. 151-74.

"The Cuyahoga River Fire: June 22, 1969." Case Western Reserve U. 25 Sept. 2002 <www.cwru.edu/artsci/engl/marling/60s/pages/richoux/index.html>.

Dunphy, Joseph. "Ecology Unit Works for Shiny, New Pennypack Creek." *The Philadelphia Inquirer* 17 Jan. 1971. North and East Delaware Valley ed.

Faill, Roger T. "Paleozoic History." *The Geology of Pennsylvania*. Ed. Charles H. Shultz. Harrisburg and Pittsburgh: Pennsylvania Geological Survey and Pittsburgh Geological Society, 1999. 418-33.

Klaric, Betty. "Stokes Promises to Lead Pollution Fight." *The Cleveland Press*. 24 June 1969: D3. Case Western Reserve U. 25 Sept. 2002.<www.cwru.edu/artsci/engl/marling/60s/pages/ richoux/Press2ndDayarticle.html>.

Laycock, George. "Invasion of the Pasture-snatcher." *Audubon* 87 (1985): 22-25.

Leopold, Aldo. *A Sand County Almanac, with Essays on Conservation from Round River*. San Francisco and New York: Sierra Club and Ballentine Books, 1966.

Lewis, Henry T. "In Retrospect." *Before the Wilderness: Environmental Management by Native Californians*. Ed. Thomas C. Blackburn and Kat Anderson. Menlo Park, California: Ballena Press, 1993. 389-400.

Lewis, Henry T. "Patterns of Indian Burning in California: Ecological Ethnohistory." *Before the Wilderness: Environmental Management by Native Californians*. Ed. Thomas C. Blackburn and Kat Anderson. Menlo Park, California: Ballena Press, 1993. 55-116.

McCarthy, Helen. "Managing Oaks and the Acorn Crop." *Before the Wilderness: Environmental Management by Native Californians*. Ed. Thomas C. Blackburn and Kat Anderson. Menlo Park, California: Ballena Press, 1993. 213-28.

MacLaughlan, David B. "Mesozoic History." *The Geology of Pennsylvania*. Ed. Charles H. Shultz. Harrisburg and Pittsburgh: Pennsylvania Geological Survey and Pittsburgh Geological Society, 1999. 434-49.

McMahon, J.J. "Train Derailed at Bryn Athyn; 4 Riders Hurt." *The Philadelphia Bulletin*. 17 March 1964:1.

McNeil, John. *Rambling along the Pennypack*. Philadelphia: Friends of Pennypack Park, 1962.

Nash, Roderick. *Wilderness and the American Mind*. 4th ed. New Haven: Yale University Press, 2001.

"Oil Slick Damages 2 River Spans." *The Plain Dealer*. 23 June 1969: C11. Case Western Reserve U. 25 Sept. 2002. <www.cwru.edu/artsci/engl/marling/60s/pages/richoux/1969PlainDealerarticle. html>.

Tilman, David, and John A. Downing. "Biodiversity and Stability in Grasslands." *Nature* 367 (1994): 363-65.

Thomas, Joseph A. *A Synopsis of the History of Upper Moreland and Willow Grove*. Willow Grove, Pennsylvania: Upper Moreland Historical Association, 2000.

Walker, Robert J. "Shelmire Mills, a Vanished Hamlet." *Old York Road Historical Society Bulletin* 52 (1992): 16-24.

Wintz, Mildred, Edward Mamorella, and Joseph A. Thomas. *Historic Mills of Moreland Township*. Willow Grove, Pennsylvania: Upper Moreland Historical Association, 1999.

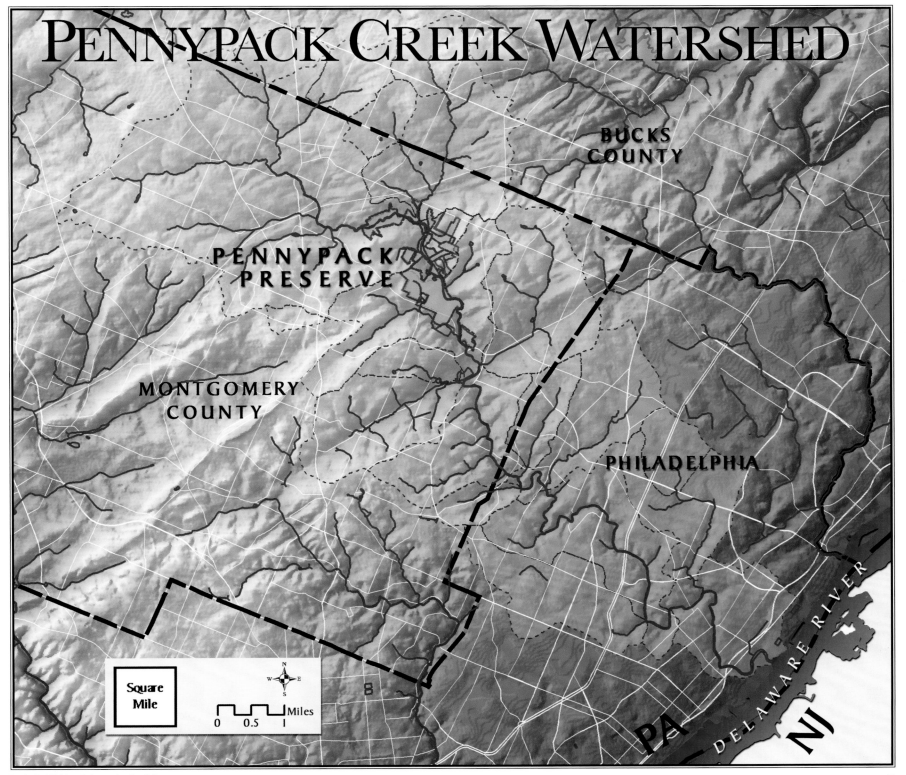

Pennypack Creek Watershed

BUCKS COUNTY

PENNYPACK PRESERVE

MONTGOMERY COUNTY

PHILADELPHIA

DELAWARE RIVER

PA

NJ

Square Mile

N W E S

Miles
0 0.5 1

Map by Chad W. Adams, Andropogon Associates, Ltd.

THIS PAGE AND OPPOSITE Turkey Vultures (*Cathartes aura*)
frequent the valley's rocky wooded slopes and quarry faces.

Great Egrets (*Ardea alba*), such as this individual in breeding plumage, are rare visitors to the preserve's wetlands.

Although never common, Red-shouldered Hawks (*Buteo lineatus*) inhabit the preserve year 'round.

THIS PAGE AND OPPPOSITE Skunk Cabbages (*Symplocarpus foetidus*) are among the earliest harbingers of spring.

Distinctive characteristics confer the common names on these spring
wildflowers: Violets (*Viola spp.*) and Bloodroot (*Sanguinaria canadensis*).

Like its habitat preference, the diet of the Eastern
Chipmunk (*Tamias striatus*) is quite varied.

Mayapples (*Podophyllus peltatum*) mostly reproduce asexually
and are very poisonous except for the occasional ripe fruit.

A Tuliptree flower (*Liriodendron tulipifera*) fallen from one of the tallest trees in the forest.

Among the more abundant birds breeding in the preserve, Mourning Doves
(*Zenaida macroura*) can be found most commonly in fencerows and woods' edges.

Eastern Garter Snakes (*Thamnophis sirtalis*) inhabit the woodlands
of the preserve, but they can be found in virtually any habitat.

The native woodland wildflower *Cimcifuga racemosa* bears a wealth of fascinating common names: Snakeroot, Black Cohosh, Bugbane, Fairy Candle and Rattletop.

A Red-shouldered Hawk (*Buteo lineatus*) scouts for prey from a perch at the edge of the forest.

Like many people, Painted Turtles (*Chrysemys picta*) cannot resist an
opportunity to sunbathe, and the activity helps keep the animals free of leeches.

Wood Ducks (*Aix sponsa*) sometimes use the wetland to raise a brood, but also seek out cavities in trees growing on the floodplain.

Birders observe Pileated Woodpeckers (*Dryocopus pileatus*)
with increasing frequency in the remnants of ancient forest.

By late summer, Green-headed Coneflowers (*Rudbeckia laciniata*) bloom in sunny patches alongside Pennypack Creek.

Solitary, secretive Green Herons (*Butorides virescens*) fish along the shores of the wetland.

Most of the time, Bullfrogs (*Rana catesbeiana*) are very wary,
but during breeding season males become far less cautious.

THIS PAGE Swamp Rose Mallow (*Hibiscus moscheutus*) and, OPPOSITE,
Red-winged Blackbirds (*Agelaius phoenciceus*) prefer open, marshy habitat.

A brood of Canada Geese (*Branta canadensis*) in the wetlands.

Stately Great Blue Herons (*Ardea herodias*) patiently
hunt a wide variety of aquatic prey in quiet waters.

Iridescent male Mallards (*Anas platyrhynchos*) in full breeding
plumage court females in aquatic habitats throughout the preserve.

Wood Ducks usually hide among vegetation at the edge of the wetland.

One pair of Canada Geese always claims the island in the wetland for breeding each year.

The fungus that produces a Satyr's Beard, *Hydnum erinaceus*, can colonize dead wood or, as in this case, a wound in a living tree.

The dramatic appearance of the edible Chicken Mushroom
(*Polyporus sulphureus*) is a sure sign of the approach of autumn.

White-breasted Nuthatches (*Sitta carolinensis*) are true conservators of the
forest as they search the bark of large, old trees for destructive insects.

During most of the year, White-tailed Deer (*Odocoileus virginianus*) live
in family groups composed of an adult doe with her fawns or yearlings.

Wild Turkeys (*Meleagris gallopavo*) released in adjacent natural areas
during the early 1990s have found ideal habitat in the Pennypack Preserve.

Yearling male Wild Turkeys remain in bachelor flocks until they are sexually mature.

Opportunistic and polygamous, the sexually mature male Wild Turkey
gobbles and struts with his fanned tail to attract and hold a harem.

Non-native Burdocks (*Arctium* spp.) disperse
by clinging to passing animals and people.

By September, when they are three months old, White-tailed
Deer fawns begin to lose their camouflaged spotted coat.

The brilliant scarlet flowers of Oswego Tea (*Monarda didyma*)
are irresistible to hummingbirds and butterflies.

Delicately fragrant Wild Blue Phlox (*Phlox divaricata*)
grace the banks of Pennypack Creek in spring.

THIS PAGE AND OPPOSITE Though lovely and attractive to pollinators, the common
non-native Musk Thistle (*Carduus nutans*) can crowd out native meadow plants.

Tree Swallows (*Tachycineta bicolor*) hawk insects over Raytharn Farm meadows.

Raytharn Farm, once a working hay farm in the midst of the Pennypack
Preserve, is gradually being transformed into a native grass meadowland.

Two denizens of hedgerows and thickets: OPPOSITE, the Northern Mockingbird
(*Mimus polyglottos*) and, THIS PAGE, the Woodchuck (*Marmota monax*).

Densely hairy, magenta canes distinguish non-native
Wineberries (*Rubus phoenicolasius*) from native raspberries.

An Eastern Tiger Swallowtail (*Papilo glaucus*) drinking nectar from a Common Milkweed (*Asclepias syriaca*) flower.

Autumn breezes catch the silky parachutes on the seeds of Common
Milkweed, spreading the plant throughout the old fields of the preserve.

Adult American Hoverflies (*Metasyrphus americanus*) pollinate flowers like Ox-eye
(*Heliopsis helianthoides*), while the predaceous larvae keep the flowers free of insect pests.